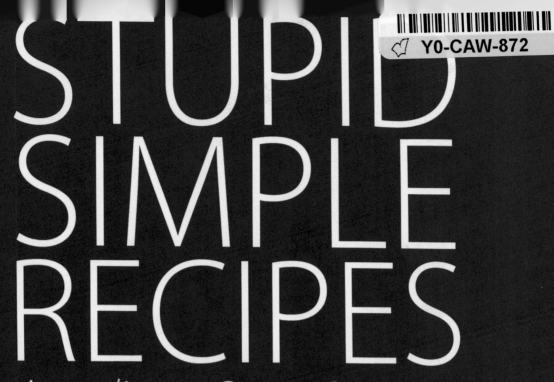

STUPID SIMPLE RECIPES

According to Cancer Survivors

The Lunch Ladies

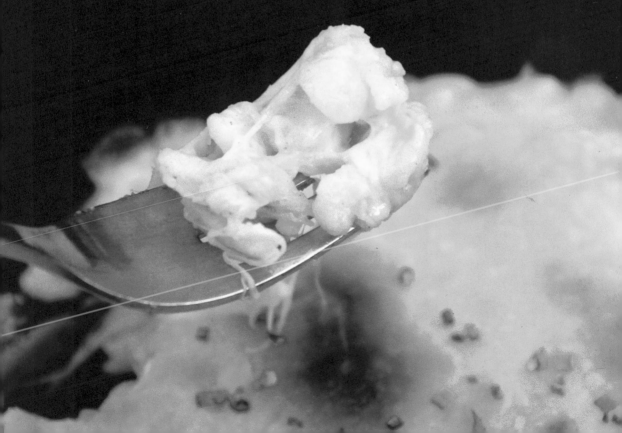

Stupid Simple Recipes
According to Cancer Survivors
All Rights Reserved.
Copyright © 2015 The Lunch Ladies
v4.0

Outskirts Press, Inc.
http://www.outskirtspress.com

ISBN: 978-1-4787-5401-5

Outskirts Press and the "OP" logo are trademarks belonging to Outskirts Press, Inc.

PRINTED IN THE UNITED STATES OF AMERICA

Our Mission Statement

We are three women who are different types of cancer survivors, breast, colon and esophageal. Starting with a dream, we became inspired to help raise money for cancer. Now we can say, we have made it a reality.

We began weekly meetings to put together recipes to create and test the simplest ways to cook meals for those with very busy schedules. We are proud to announce that this is our first edition of many cookbooks that we are planning to publish for cancer research.

We are dedicated to helping all that are in the battle and pride ourselves on raising funds to FADE THE COLORS OF CANCER. Our mission is to have people become aware of the many cancers people are battling today and our goal is to raise money to help support in any way we can. We will as a group participate in walks, volunteer at hospital cancer units for chemo patients and raise money with special events, donating 25% of our proceeds to cancer research. We are "The Lunch Ladies LLC" and we are determined to...FADE THE COLORS OF CANCER.

Visit our website at: www.fadethecolors.com

Meet the Lunch Ladies

Ilene Vazquez

"What doesn't kill you makes you stronger, stand a little taller"....My name is Ilene Vazquez and I am a Colon Cancer survivor. My last chemotherapy treatment was on 12/31/13 and that date is now tattooed on my chest, covering the scar where my port for chemo treatment once was.

I am very lucky to have had the best medical team with Mount Kisco Medical Group, including my general physician Dr. Rizzi and his staff, my surgeon Dr. Messina and her staff, my Gastroenterologist Dr. Close and her staff and my Oncologist Dr. Gold and her staff. I'd like to especially thank all the nurses that work for these doctors, they are truly amazing!

I would also like to thank all my family, especially my husband David and my sons Jake and Nico. In addition I would like to say to all my friends and family who visited me in the hospital and at my home that helped tremendously through this whole ordeal..."I will NEVER forget what you did for me".

I am a strong believer that giving back is something we all must do. Not only giving back to those who helped us but for all cancer patients who are currently battling.

So after plenty of thought on how I could give back I finally came up with what I want to do. I am a cooking instructor/caterer and have many simple recipes to share. With every recipe in this book each dish represents a new creation of hope for current cancer patients.

Whether you are cooking for your own family or someone else's I think you will appreciate these simple and delicious recipes. Thank you for buying this book and for helping to support cancer awareness and research.

Jill K. Vallaro

I am Jill Vallaro and I was diagnosed with esophageal cancer in May of 2011. Although I thought my life was over, I found it was just the beginning of my stronger one. After all of my chemotherapy, radiation and surgery, I realized how blessed I was to have such wonderful support from my family and my medical team at New York Presbyterian Hospital. I received the gift of a second chance.

Therefore, I felt it was only proper to dedicate this book to my family, my husband Ron, my daughter Carisa, my son-in-law Bruce and my grandson, Jake; my New York Presbyterian medical team, Dr. Joshua Sonett, and staff, and Dr. Mark Stoopler and staff. Thank you all for giving me the strength and support to carry me through my treatment and recovery so I can remain cancer free. Also, to all of my good friends, without you I would have fallen to pieces. You kept me strong and positive through long hours and sometimes days of difficult recovery. My main focus became my new grandson who was only one week old when I was diagnosed with cancer. I needed to be there for him. I knew I had to fight.

Being three years cancer free, I feel it is time to give back to those who are going through the battle as I did and hope I can make their fight easier. With the help of two other amazing women, the three of us have braved our fight and won and now we will fight for others who need us.

Yvette Delgado

My name is Yvette Delgado, fifteen years ago at the age of 30, I was diagnosed with this terrible illness Breast cancer. Most people at this age would have thought it was the worst thing that could have happened to them. I was young my life was just beginning to be shaped around what I wanted. To say overcoming something as horrible as this at that age or even understanding how real it was at the time is something I would never classify as easy. I cried, I thought of the worst possible outcomes, but what I took away from that time was that it was still my reality. I had a disease that is so devastating. So, I put it to the challenge with Gods help to survive breast cancer, and here I am today telling you that this is why for me it was the best year of my life. Not only did that year open my eyes to what life has to give and how much of life people take for granted, it also gave me the achievement of survival.

Surviving such a devastating disease is something you walk away from being more then blessed. It would be selfish on my part to just live the rest of my life as if I have never went through this time battling cancer. I figured this is a message from above to not only live life with a different and more meaningful view, but to give back to those who fought for me. Cancer is an internal war and It is a war that is fought with more emotional and mental strength then physical. I am giving back not for myself, not because I feel compelled to, but because it's the least I can do for those who fought for me and cheered me on through the hardest times. For me being so young at the time, my team of nurses and my family and close friends were my support who gave me more than just hope in myself, but they gave me the confidence to overcome something that can seem impossible at times. To say I'm blessed is an understatement. That is why I am giving back now and why it is so important to me and the two ladies alongside me. Just as in life's spectrum it's essential to stay healthy, strong and courageous.

Welcome to our kitchen

1. Breakfast
    -   Broccoli and Spinach Stromboli.........................9
    -   Oven Baked French Toast with Orange Sauce.............41
    -   Corn and Asparagus Frittata..........................16

2. Appetizers
    -   Crockpot Creamy Chicken Dip..........................20
    -   Black Bean and Corn Salsa.............................8
    -   Asian Chicken Wings...................................2
    -   Spinach Fritters.....................................49
    -   Fried Wontons..25
    -   Meatballs..36
    -   Shrimp Ceviche.......................................45

3. Soups
    -   Crockpot Split Pea Soup..............................22
    -   Crockpot Chicken Noodle Soup.........................19
    -   Crockpot Minestrone Soup.............................21
    -   Meatball Soup..35

4. Salads
    -   Caesar Salad...11
    -   Apple Spinach Salad...................................1
    -   No Mayo Chicken Salad................................40
    -   Crab and Mango Salad.................................17
    -   Pear & Gorgonzola Salad..............................42

5. Main Meals
    -   Pork Chops and Sweet Peppers.........................43
    -   Chicken with Apples and Spinach......................14
    -   Chile Sandwich.......................................15
    -   Lemon Pasta..32
    -   Italian Fried Steak..................................29
    -   Mexican Chicken and Cornbread........................37
    -   Sloppy Joes..47
    -   Italian Meatloaves...................................30
    -   Cheesy Chicken.......................................12
    -   Mexican Chorizo and Rice.............................38
    -   Ginger Honey Salmon..................................26

- Mexican Lasagna 39
- Margarita Spaghetti 34
- Spaghetti and Shrimp 48
- Balsamic Sauce over Flank Steak 5
- Chicken Piccata 13
- Baked Flounder 4
- Asparagus and Pesto Pizza 3

6. Sides
- Easy Potatoes 23
- Cooked Sweet Kale 31
- Brussels with Balsamic 10
- Rice and Gandules 44
- Mac and Cheese 33

7. Desserts
- Healthy Pumpkin Pudding 28
- Very Berry Pie 50
- Fried Bananas 24
- Crack Bites 18
- White Chocolate Meringue Drops 51

8. Drinks
- Green Tea 27
- Banana Pineapple Mango Rum 6
- Simple Punch 46
- Beer Mojito 7

Apple Spinach Salad

Yield: 4 Servings
Cooking Time: 20 minutes

1 tablespoon lemon juice	**2 apples, skinned, cored and sliced**
1 tablespoon extra-virgin olive oil	**½ onion, sliced thin**
1 tablespoon honey	**3 cups fresh spinach**
¼ teaspoon salt	**¼ cup craisins**

Whisk together the lemon juice, oil, honey and salt in a salad bowl.

Add the apples, onion slices and spinach and toss.

Top with craisins and toss again.

Asian Chicken Wings

Yield: 4 Servings
Cooking Time: 30 minutes
Marinating Time: 2 hours

2 lbs. chicken wings
½ cup soy sauce
¼ teaspoon ground ginger
2 tablespoons fresh cilantro, chopped
2 cloves garlic, chopped

1 tablespoon lemon juice
2 tablespoon butter (unsalted)
¼ cup honey
Sesame seeds for garnish

Put wings into a gallon size Ziploc bag for marinating. In a small bowl whisk together the soy sauce, ginger, cilantro, garlic and lemon juice. Add mixture to wings in Ziploc bag and refrigerate for at least 2 hours.

Heat butter in a large skillet over medium high heat. When the butter melts add the honey and turn the heat up to high.

Place wings and marinade in the skillet. Leave the heat on high and turn every 5 minutes for a total of 20-30 minutes or until liquid is reduced onto the wings in a sticky consistency and the wings are brown and cooked through.

Garnish with sesame seeds.

Asparagus and Pesto Pizza

Yield: 1 Pizza
Cooking Time: 15 minutes

1 cup prepared jar pesto
½ lb. asparagus spears, trimmed
   and chopped in 1 inch pieces
12 inch prepared pizza piecrust

½ lb. Fontina cheese,
   cut into small pieces
1 cup cherry tomatoes, halved

Preheat oven to 425 degrees.

Boil a ½ inch of water in a medium skillet. Place asparagus in the boiling water and cover. Steam until just tender (about 4 minutes). Drain the asparagus with very cold water, to stop the cooking process.

Spread the pesto sauce on top of the pizza crust evenly in one flat layer.

Combine the steamed asparagus, fontina cheese and cherry tomatoes in a medium size bowl and spoon on top of the pesto sauce.

Bake for about 10 minutes on the middle rack, or until the cheese is fully melted.

Let stand for about 5 minutes before slicing.

Baked Flounder

Yield: 4 Servings
Cooking Time: 30 minutes

1lb. Flounder Fillets
1 tablespoon unsalted butter
Salt and pepper to taste

1 tablespoon lemon juice
1 teaspoon dried basil
½ teaspoon garlic powder

Preheat oven to 350 degrees.

Spray a baking dish with non-stick cooking spray and arrange flounder in dish. Dot each piece with butter and season with salt and pepper. Sprinkle with lemon juice.

Top with basil and garlic powder and cover. Bake for 30 minutes.

Balsamic Sauce over Flank Steak

Yield: 4 Servings
Cooking Time: 25 minutes

1 flank steak
Salt and pepper
1 tablespoon extra-virgin olive oil

Balsamic Sauce:
4 cloves garlic, chopped
½ cup balsamic vinegar
3 tablespoons honey
2 tablespoons extra-virgin olive oil
1 tablespoon Dijon mustard

Heat a grill pan on high heat. Season steak with salt, pepper and oil (brush it on both sides). Sear steak for 2 minutes on each side. Turn heat down to medium and continue to cook for 20 minutes, 10 minutes on each side.

In the meantime, whisk all the ingredients for the balsamic sauce in a small bowl. Heat in small pan for 5 minutes until bubbly.

When steak is done, remove from grill and allow to rest for 5 minutes. Slice steak against the grain (the lines in the steak). Arrange on serving plate. Pour balsamic sauce over sliced steak.

Suggestion: Serve with any green vegetable by pouring sauce over vegetable and steak.

Banana Pineapple Mango Rum

Yield: 4 Servings
Cooking Time: 5 minutes

2 bananas
½ cup crushed pineapple with juice
1 cup frozen mango

15 oz. can coconut cream
3 oz. rum

Put all ingredients except the rum and ice to fill blender and blend until smooth.

Add rum and stir.

Beer Mojito

Yield: 1 Serving
Cooking Time: 5 minutes

1 shot Vodka
½ bottle Apple/Ginger Beer
1 teaspoon Lime juice

Sprig of Mint
Ice

Fill a glass with ice and add all ingredients. Stir to combine.

Black Bean and Corn Salsa

Yield: 4-6 Servings
Cooking Time: 15 minutes

1 cup chunky style salsa
  (mild, medium or hot)
¼ cup extra virgin olive oil
Pinch of Salt & pepper

15 oz. can black beans,
  drained & rinsed
2 cups frozen corn, defrosted
1 handful fresh cilantro, chopped

In a medium size bowl, whisk the ingredients together for the dressing, the salsa, oil, salt & pepper.

Add the beans, corn and cilantro on top of the dressing. Stir all ingredients together in the bowl and serve.

Broccoli and Spinach Stromboli

Yield: 4 Servings
Cooking Time: 30 minutes

4 eggs	**2 cloves garlic, minced**
½ teaspoon salt	**13.8 oz. package refrigerated**
¼ teaspoon pepper	**pizza dough**
2 tablespoons extra virgin olive oil	**1 ½ cups fresh spinach**
3 ounces chopped broccoli florets	**¼ cup fresh basil, chopped**
1 onion, chopped	**¼ cup grated parmesan cheese, divided**

Preheat oven to 400 degrees. In a medium bowl whisk together the eggs, salt and pepper and set aside.

Heat the oil in a large skillet over medium high heat. Add the broccoli and onions, saute for about 4 minutes. Add garlic and cook for 1 more minute.

Turn heat down to medium and pour in egg mixture and continue cooking until egg mixture is cooked through but is still glossy and moist.

Unroll pizza dough and shape into and even 14x9 inch rectangle, stretching slightly. Arrange spinach over dough. Sprinkle with basil and 2 tablespoons of the cheese and spoon egg mixture evenly over dough. Starting at the short side, carefully roll up dough around filling. Pinch seam and ends to seal.

Place roll on nonstick prepared baking sheet. Brush roll with remaining 1 tablespoon oil and sprinkle with remaining cheese. Using a sharp knife, make diagonal slashes on top of roll at about 1 ½ inch intervals.

Bake for about 15 minutes or until golden.

Brussels with Balsamic

Yield: 4 Servings
Cooking Time: 30 minutes

16 ounce bag frozen Brussel Sprouts,
   defrosted
2 tablespoons extra virgin olive oil

1 ½ tablespoons balsamic vinegar
½ teaspoon salt

Preheat oven to 400 degrees.

Cut each Brussel sprout in half and place in a medium bowl. Add the oil, vinegar and salt and toss to combine.

Place brussel sprouts on baking sheet and bake in oven for 30 minutes.

Caesar Salad

Yield: 4 Servings
Cooking Time: 15 minutes

½ cup lite mayo
2 tablespoons lemon juice
2 tablespoons worcestershire sauce
1 teaspoon garlic powder

Pinch of salt and pepper
1 cup shredded Parmesan cheese
10 oz. bag chopped Romaine lettuce
3 cups croutons

Whisk mayo, lemon juice, Worcestershire, garlic powder, salt and pepper together in a large bowl.

Add parmesan cheese, lettuce and croutons and do not toss until ready to serve. Store in fridge until ready.

Cheesy Chicken

Yield: 4 Servings
Cooking Time: 45 minutes
Marinating Time: 2 hours

1 ½ lbs. chicken tenders cut in 1 inch pieces

2 beaten eggs

1 cup seasoned breadcrumbs

2 cloves garlic, peeled and chopped

6 tablespoons extra virgin olive oil, divided

2 cubes chicken bouillon dissolved in 1 cup of water

1 ½ cups Muenster cheese, shredded

Marinate chicken in eggs for at least two hours, then drain. DO NOT RINSE.

Preheat oven to 350 degrees.

Mix breadcrumbs and garlic together in shallow dish. Using a slotted spoon, remove chicken from egg and coat in batches in breadcrumbs.

Heat large skillet with 2 tablespoons of oil. On medium high heat brown chicken in oil about 5 minutes turning often. Again, do this in batches so that you have room in skillet for chicken to brown. Once each batch is done put into an ovenproof casserole dish.

Pour dissolved bullion on top of cooked chicken in casserole dish. Cover with cheese evenly. Cover and bake for 35 minutes.

Serve over white rice.

Chicken Piccata

Yield: 4 Servings
Cooking Time: 25 minutes

2 lbs. (or 3 thick) skinless and boneless chicken breasts, cut into thin cutlets	**½ lemon-juiced**
	2 cups chicken broth
Salt & pepper	**1-3 ¼ oz. jar of capers, drained**
Flour, for dredging	**and rinsed**
5 tablespoons unsalted butter	**Fresh parsley for garnish**
6 tablespoons extra-virgin olive oil	

Season the chicken with salt and pepper on both sides. Dredge chicken in flour and shake off the excess.

In a large skillet over medium high heat, melt 2 tablespoons of butter with 3 tablespoons of olive oil. When the butter is melted add 3 pieces of chicken and cook on each side for 3 minutes per side (just to brown). Remove and transfer to plate. Melt 2 more tablespoons of butter and another 2 tablespoons of olive oil. Add the other 3 pieces of chicken and brown in the same manner (3 minutes per side). Remove from pan and add to plate.

Add the lemon juice, stock and capers to pan. Bring to boil, scraping up all the brown bits from the bottom of the pan. Check the seasoning. Return all the chicken to the pan and simmer for 5 minutes. Remove the chicken to a platter. Add the remaining one tablespoon of butter and whisk in sauce. Pour sauce over chicken and garnish with parsley.

Chicken with Apples and Spinach

Yield: 4 Servings
Cooking Time: 30 minutes

4 thin cut chicken breasts	**¼ cup honey**
1 cup Italian breadcrumbs	**2 tablespoons Dijon mustard**
2 eggs, beaten	**2 tablespoons cider vinegar**
¼ teaspoon salt	**2 medium apples, cored and sliced**
2 tablespoons extra virgin olive oil	**6 cups fresh spinach**

Put breadcrumbs in a shallow dish for breading and egg and salt in a separate shallow dish for breading. Dip each chicken breast in the egg and then breadcrumbs to coat.

Heat oil in a large skillet on medium high heat. Cook breaded chicken for 5 minutes on each side. Remove from pan onto separate dish.

Stir honey, mustard, and vinegar into the drippings in skillet. Add apple slices and cook for about 4 minutes or until crisp tender. Add in spinach and a pinch of salt. Let cook for 2 more minutes, or until spinach is wilted.

Place apple and spinach mixture over chicken and serve.

Chile Sandwich

Yield: 4 Servings
Cooking Time: 15 minutes

1 ½ lbs. flank steak
1 teaspoon adobo seasoning
2 garlic cloves, minced
2 tablespoons extra virgin olive oil
2 ripe avocados
1 tablespoon lime juice

¼ teaspoon salt
1 jalapeno, deseeded and chopped
4 soft Kaiser rolls
1 tomato, sliced
4 slices Muenster cheese

Place steak in a re-sealable bag and add adobo, garlic and oil. Place in refrigerator for one hour.

Grill steaks 6 to 10 minutes per side.

Mash avocado with lime juice, salt and jalapeno.

Assemble the sandwich using the rolls, tomato, cheese, meat and avocado mixture.

Corn and Asparagus Frittata

Yield: 4 Servings
Cooking Time: 30 minutes

2 tablespoons extra-virgin olive oil	¼ teaspoon paprika
1 cup frozen corn kernels (defrosted)	Non-stick cooking spray
1 bunch asparagus, trimmed and chopped	¼ cup low fat milk
2 shallots, diced	6 eggs, lightly beaten
½ teaspoon salt	Salt and pepper to taste
¼ teaspoon pepper	1 cup shredded Mexican cheese blend

Preheat oven to 350 degrees.

Heat oil in a large ovenproof skillet over medium high heat.

Add corn, asparagus and shallots to heated skillet and saute for 5 minutes, stirring frequently. Stir in salt, pepper and the paprika. Place corn mixture in a bowl to cool.

Spray skillet with nonstick cooking spray.

Whisk together the eggs, milk, salt and pepper in a medium size bowl. Add in corn mixture and stir to combine. Return mixture to skillet and cook 4 minutes without stirring. Cover and reduce heat to medium low and cook 10 minutes or until eggs are set.

Sprinkle cheese evenly over eggs. Bake for 4-5 minutes in preheated oven, until cheese is melted.

Crab and Mango Salad

Yield: 4 Servings
Cooking Time: 10 minutes

1 lb. crab meat, cut in 1 inch pieces
1 ripe mango, cut in 1 inch pieces
1 jalapeño, deseeded and chopped
2 tablespoons extra virgin olive oil

Pinch of salt and pepper to taste
2 tablespoons lime juice
1 bunch cilantro, chopped

Put all ingredients in medium bowl and mix to combine.

Crack Bites

Yield: 8-10 Servings
Cooking Time: 20 minutes

1 loaf of white bread
2 cups of sugar
2 tablespoons cinnamon

1 stick butter
16 oz. container of whipped cream
   cheese

Preheat oven to 350 degrees.

On a cutting board, lay one slice of white bread and roll until flattened thin. Repeat with all slices. Spread all the slices of bread with a thin layer of cream cheese.

Combine the sugar and cinnamon in a plate. Melt the butter in a separate shallow dish for dipping the bread.

Roll each bread slice up and dip in melted butter and then in the sugar and cinnamon mixture and place on a cookie sheet prepared with nonstick spray.

Bake for 15 minutes. When done allow to cool and slice each roll in bite size pieces.

Crockpot Chicken Noodle Soup

Yield: 6-8 Servings
Cooking Time: 6 hours-high

1 large onion, chopped

3 stalks celery, chopped

4 carrots, peeled and chopped

8 frozen skinless, boneless chicken
  thighs, cut in 1 inch pieces

8 cups chicken broth

½ teaspoon salt

½ teaspoon adobo seasoning

½ box small pasta, cooked according
  to box directions.

Put all ingredients into crockpot. Turn crockpot on high setting. Cook for 5-6 hours until carrots are tender.

Add cooked pasta before serving.

Crockpot Creamy Chicken Dip

Yield: 8-10 Servings
Cooking Time: 4 hours/crockpot

4 frozen chicken breasts
15oz. can black beans, rinsed and
  drained

1 ½ cups frozen corn
2 cups mild chunky salsa
4 oz. cream cheese

Put all ingredients except for the cream cheese in the crockpot and cook on high for 4 hours.

Shred chicken with a fork and add the cream cheese. Stir to combine.

Serve with chips.

Crockpot Minestrone Soup

Yield: 8 Servings
Cooking Time: 6 hours

8 oz. package dried cannellini beans
1 large onion, chopped
2 stalks celery, chopped
2 cups baby carrots, halved
2 tbsp. minced garlic
1 tsp. Italian seasoning

8 cups chicken broth
1 lb. boneless ham steak-
   cut in 1" pieces
14.5 oz. can diced tomatoes, with juice
14.5 oz. can kale
½ box spaghetti, cut into pieces

Put all ingredients except for spaghetti into crockpot and stir. Cook on high for 6 or hours, or until carrots and beans are soft.

Meanwhile, cook spaghetti according to box directions and serve soup with some cut spaghetti.

Crockpot Split Pea Soup

Yield: 6-8 Servings
Cooking Time: 6-8 hours-Low

1 lb. green split peas, rinsed and drained

1 large leek, white and light green part only, halved lengthwise and thinly sliced crosswise

2 stalks celery, chopped

2 carrots, chopped

½ tsp. dried parsley

½ tsp. dried thyme

½ tsp. salt

½ tsp. pepper

½ lb. ham, chopped into ½ pieces

4 cups beef broth

4 cups water

Place split peas, leek, celery, carrots, parsley, thyme, salt and pepper in crockpot and stir to combine. Add the ham, broth and water and stir again. Cover and cook on low 6-8 hours.

Notes: If soup sits for a while before serving and becomes a little thick, add some water and stir.

Easy Potatoes

Yield: 4 Servings
Cooking Time: 25 minutes

3 potatoes, peeled and sliced very thin   **1 teaspoon Salt**
2 tablespoons extra virgin olive oil   **⅛ teaspoon Pepper**
1 tablespoon Italian Seasoning   **½ cup shredded Parmesan Cheese**
½ teaspoon minced garlic

Preheat oven to 450 degrees.

Toss together the potatoes, oil, Italian seasoning, minced garlic, salt and pepper in a medium size bowl.

Put potatoes on a baking sheet prepared with non-stick cooking spray in an even layer.

Bake for 20 minutes. Top evenly with cheese and bake for 5 more minutes.

Fried Bananas

Yield: 4 Servings
Cooking Time: 15 mins.

2 tbsp. of Butter   **½ teaspoon of Vanilla**
¼ cup of Light Brown Sugar   **2 bananas**
½ teaspoon of cinnamon

In a frying pan melt butter, light brown sugar, cinnamon and vanilla on low heat.

Slice Bananas in half and add to the pan for 3-4 minutes on each side.

Serve with ice cream.

Fried Wontons

Yield: 6 Servings
Cooking Time: 30 minutes

1 Package of wonton pasta
1 lb. of ground pork meat
1 egg
1 teaspoon salt

1 tbsp. of chopped ginger
2 thinly chopped scallions
1 cup of oil to deep fry

Mix ground pork, egg yolk only, salt, ginger and scallion together.

Remove wonton pasta by slice and fill in mixture. Fold wonton in half like triangle to close and fold over again. Use egg white to stick corners together. Let it sit and dry for about an hour. Heat up oil and fry until golden brown. Use duck sauce to dip.

Ginger Honey Salmon

Yield: 4 Servings
Cooking Time: 15 minutes

2 tablespoons extra virgin olive oil   **⅛ cup honey**
6 skinless salmon fillets   **4 tablespoons soy sauce**
1 teaspoon grated fresh ginger   **2 tablespoons sesame seeds**

Heat oil in a large skillet over medium high heat. Cook Salmon fillets for about 4-5 minutes per side. Remove out of skillet onto a plate.

In a small bowl whisk together the ginger, honey and soy sauce.

In same skillet add the soy sauce mixture and bring to a boil for about 2 minutes.

Add back to the skillet the salmon fillets and cook for another minute to warm through in the sauce.

Sprinkle with sesame seeds and serve with rice or in a salad.

Green Tea

Yield: 4 Servings
Cooking Time: 5 minutes

32 oz. Bottle Arizona Green Tea
   with Ginseng and Honey
8 Mint Leaves
2 Lemon Wedges

Ice

Optional: 1 Shot per 8 ounces of
   Spiced Rum

Put all ingredients except the rum in a pitcher and stir to combine.

Add rum if desired and stir.

Healthy Pumpkin Pudding

Yield: 5 Servings
Preparation Time: 10 minutes. 2 hours refrigeration time

4 bananas   **1 ½ teaspoons pumpkin pie spice**
1 cup pumpkin puree   **5 ginger snap cookies**
1/3 cup honey   **Optional: whip cream**

Place first four ingredients in a blender and blend.

Divide equally into 5 small serving cups and insert cookie in each.

Refrigerate for 2 hours before serving. Top with whip cream if desired.

Italian Fried Steak

Yield: 4 Servings
Cooking Time: 25 minutes

½ cup Italian seasoned breadcrumbs
½ cup shredded Parmesan cheese,
  divided
1 egg, lightly beaten
2 tablespoons water
4 beef cube steaks (.75 lbs. total, if one
  large piece cut into fillets)

Salt and pepper to taste
2 tablespoons extra virgin olive oil
12 ounce jar roasted red sweet
  peppers, drained
8 fresh basil leaves, chopped
¼ teaspoon garlic powder
Salt and pepper to taste

In a shallow dish for breading mix the bread crumbs and half of the cheese. In another shallow dish for breading mix the egg and water.

Season each steak with salt and pepper. Dip each steak in the egg mixture and then the breadcrumbs, turning once and pressing lightly to coat.

Heat the oil in a large skillet over medium high heat. Cook steaks for 5 minutes each side.

Meanwhile combine the roasted peppers, remaining cheese, basil leaves and garlic powder in a food processor and process until smooth. Season mixture with salt and pepper to taste. Transfer mixture to hot skillet with the steaks. Cover and cook on low 5 more minutes to heat through.

Italian Meatloaves

Yield: 4 Servings
Cooking Time: 30 minutes

1 egg, lightly beaten
¾ cup prepared pasta sauce, ¼ cup
   extra sauce for tops of meat loafs
½ cup Italian style breadcrumbs
¼ cup fresh basil leaves, chopped

¼ teaspoon salt
1 pound ground turkey
8 ounce block Mozzarella cheese, cut
  in 1 inch pieces

Preheat oven to 450 degrees. Spray medium baking sheet with non-stick spray.

In a large bowl combine the egg, pasta sauce, basil and salt. Add the ground turkey, breadcrumbs, cheese and mix well.

Using a ½ size measuring cup, make oval shaped meatloaves and line on prepared baking sheet. Brush the top of each meatloaf with the remaining ¼ cup of pasta sauce.

Bake for about 20 minutes or until meat is cooked through.

Cooked Sweet Kale

Yield: 4 Servings
Cooking Time: 15 minutes

2 tablespoons extra virgin olive oil	**Pinch of black pepper**
1 onion, chopped	**1 cup chicken stock**
2 cloves garlic, chopped	**8 ounces fresh kale**
2 tablespoons Dijon mustard	**½ cup craisins**
½ tablespoons sugar	**¼ cup sliced almonds**
1 tablespoon cider vinegar	
Pinch of Kosher salt	

Heat the oil in a large skillet over medium high heat. Add the onion and saute for 5 minutes. Add garlic and continue to saute for 1 more minute.

Add mustard, sugar, cider vinegar, salt, pepper, chicken stock and water and bring to a boil.

Add Kale, mix and cover. Cook covered for about 5 minutes, stirring frequently.

Add craisins and continue cooking uncovered for 5 more minutes.

Turn off heat and mix in almonds.

Lemon Pasta

Yield: 4 Servings
Cooking Time: 30 minutes

1 pound Spaghetti	10 ounce bag fresh spinach
2 tablespoons unsalted butter	1 tablespoon lemon juice
3 cloves garlic, chopped	½ teaspoon salt
1 cup chicken broth	¼ teaspoon pepper
¼ cup fresh parsley, chopped	¼ cup grated parmesan cheese
1 bunch asparagus, trimmed and cut into 1 inch pieces	

Cook pasta according to box directions.

Heat a large skillet over medium high heat. Melt the butter. Add the garlic and cook for 1 minute. Add the chicken broth and parsley and bring to boil.

Add the asparagus and bring to another boil. Add spinach and lemon juice and cook until spinach is wilted, tossing frequently, about 3 minutes. Add salt and pepper to taste. Add drained cooked pasta to skillet and toss with asparagus/spinach mixture.

Add cheese and serve.

Mac and Cheese

Yield: 6 Servings
Cooking Time: 35 minutes

1 lb. macaroni pasta, cooked according to box directions

8 oz. Monterey Jack Cheese, cut up in 1 inch pieces

8 oz. Mild Cheddar Cheese, cut up in 1 inch pieces

8 oz. Gouda Cheese, cut up in 1 inch pieces

¼ cup light cream

¼ teaspoon pepper

Preheat oven to 350 degrees.

Mix all ingredients and bake in a large nonstick baking dish. Bake for 30 minutes or until cheese is melted.

Margarita Spaghetti

Yield: 4 Servings
Cooking Time: 20 minutes

1 box spaghetti
2 tablespoons extra virgin olive oil
1 onion, chopped
4 cloves garlic, minced
½ pint cherry tomatoes, halved
½ teaspoon salt

¼ teaspoon pepper
¼ cup shredded fresh basil
1 block Mozzarella cheese cut in
** 1 inch cubes**
½ cup shredded parmesan cheese
** to taste**

Cook pasta according to box directions.

Heat the oil in a large skillet over medium high heat. Add onion and saute for 5 minutes. Add garlic and cook for another minute. Stir in tomatoes, salt and pepper and cook for 3 more minutes.

Combine sauce with cooked pasta and add mozzarella cheese, parm cheese and basil. Serve cold or hot.

Meatball Soup

Yield: 4-6 Servings
Cooking Time: 40 minutes

12 cups chicken broth	**½ cup parmesan cheese**
1 ½ pounds ground beef	**¼ teaspoon pepper**
1 onion, shredded or grated	**1 box frozen spinach, do not thaw**
1 handful fresh parsley, chopped	
1 large clove garlic, minced	**For the Egg Drop:**
1 teaspoon salt	**2 eggs**
1 egg	**2 tablespoons parmesan cheese**

Bring chicken broth to a boil in a large soup pot.

Meanwhile in a medium bowl, combine the ground meat, onion, parsley, garlic, salt, egg, parmesan cheese and pepper and combine. Make small balls, about 1 inch in diameter and drop in boiling chicken broth.

Add the frozen spinach into chicken broth and simmer for about 15 minutes.

In a small bowl, combine the eggs and cheese and whisk to combine. With a fork stir the soup constantly while adding the egg mixture. Egg will immediately break up and cook all throughout the soup. Continue to cook soup at a simmer for another 5 minutes.

Meatballs

Yield: 4 Servings
Cooking Time: 1 hour

2 tablespoons extra virgin olive oil   **8 ounce can ginger ale**
1 bag of your favorite frozen meatballs,   **1 cup ketchup**
   defrosted or make your own.

In a deep frying pan heat pan with oil and braise meatballs.

Add ginger ale and ketchup. Cover and leave on low heat for 1 hour.

Mexican Chicken and Cornbread

Yield: 4 Servings
Cooking Time: 20 minutes

1 Cooked Rotisserie Chicken, skinned, pulled off bone and chopped into 1 inch pieces

2 cups prepared salsa, mild and chunky

15 ounce can red kidney beans (rinsed and drained)

1 teaspoon chili powder

2/3 cup water

8.5 ounce package corn bread mix

1 egg

¼ cup water

In a large deep skillet combine the chicken, salsa, beans, chili powder and water. Bring to a boil.

Meanwhile in a medium bowl whisk together the cornbread mix, egg and the water. Pour mixture over boiling chicken mixture in skillet.

Reduce heat to medium high and cook covered for 15 minutes.

Chorizo and Rice

Yield: 4 Servings
Cooking Time: 25 minutes

2 tablespoons extra virgin olive oil
1 lb. Chorizo, cut into 1 inch pieces
2 cups frozen Kale
14.5 oz. can diced tomatoes, undrained
1 cup uncooked instant rice
½ cup water

2 teaspoons chili powder
½ teaspoon cumin
Salt and pepper to taste
15 oz. can pinto beans, rinsed
   and drained
½ cup Mexican blend shredded cheese

Heat the oil in a large skillet on medium high heat. Add chorizo and cook for about 5 minutes.

Add kale, tomatoes, rice, water, chili powder, cumin, salt and pepper and bring to a boil.

Cover and reduce heat to a simmer. Cook covered for about 10 minutes, until liquid is absorbed and rice is tender.

Stir in beans and cook 2 more minutes just to heat through. Turn off heat, top with cheese and let sit covered for another 2 minutes, until cheese is melted.

Mexican Lasagna

Yield: 4 Servings
Cooking Time: 15 minutes

1 Cooked Rotisserie Chicken, skinned, pulled off bone and chopped into 1 inch pieces

16 oz. jar medium chunky Southwestern style salsa

3 large tortillas, each cut in half to make 6 pieces

1 ½ cups Mexican shredded cheese

6 oz. can black olives, chopped

Preheat oven to 325 degrees.

In a large deep skillet combine the chicken and salsa and cook on medium high for about 5 minutes or until heated through.

Spray a lasagna dish with non-stick cooking spray. Line the bottom with 3 pieces of tortilla. Spoon the chicken and salsa mixture on top evenly. Top with the three remaining tortilla pieces. Top with cheese and then olives evenly. Cover and cook for about 10 minutes until cheese is melted.

No Mayo Chicken Salad

Yield: 2 Servings
Cooking Time: 15 minutes

1 teaspoon mustard

1 tablespoon Balsamic vinegar

3 tablespoons extra-virgin olive oil

12.5 oz. can chicken breast packed in water, drained

Salt & pepper to taste

2 vine ripe tomatoes, seeded & chopped

2 tablespoons fresh basil leaves, chopped

In a medium size bowl, whisk together the mustard, balsamic vinegar, olive oil and salt and pepper.

Add the chicken, tomatoes and basil and stir to combine.

Oven Baked French Toast
with Orange Sauce

Yield: 4 Servings
Cooking Time: 20 minutes

2 eggs	**½ cup orange juice**
2 egg whites	**2 tablespoon honey**
1 ½ cups lowfat milk	**1 heaping teaspoon cornstarch**
2 teaspoons Vanilla	**¼ teaspoon cinnamon**
1 tablespoon cinnamon	**Powdered sugar to sprinkle**
8 slices of 1 inch thick Challah bread	

Preheat oven to 450 degrees. Spray medium baking sheet with non-stick spray liberally.

In a pie plate whisk the eggs, egg whites, milk, vanilla and cinnamon. Dip the bread slices, 2 at a time, in mixture on each side. Arrange on baking sheet.

Bake for 6 minutes, turn bread over and bake for an additional 5 minutes.

Meanwhile for syrup, combine the orange juice, honey, cornstarch and cinnamon in a small saucepot. Cook and whisk on medium high heat until thickened and bubbly. Cook for 2 minutes until thickened.

Top French toast with orange syrup and powdered sugar.

Pear & Gorgonzola Salad

Yield: 4 Servings
Cooking Time: 10 minutes

10 oz. bag of mixed greens   **⅓ cup sliced almonds**
¼ cup craisins   **1 pear, sliced thin**
3 ounces crumbled gorgonzola cheese   **¼ cup dressing of choice**

Combine all ingredients in a large salad bowl, toss and serve.

Pork Chops and Sweet Peppers

Yield: 4 Servings
Cooking Time: 30 minutes

1 tablespoon butter	**2 cloves garlic, sliced**
2 tablespoons extra virgin olive oil	**1 shallot, chopped**
4 bone in center cut pork chops	**1 large jar red sweet peppers**
Salt and pepper	

Melt butter and oil in a large skillet on medium high heat.

Season pork shops with salt and pepper and fry on each side for about 2 minutes. Remove from skillet.

Add garlic and shallots to skillet and saute for about 5 minutes. Add the pork chops back to skillet. Add the sweet peppers and half the jar of the juice from the peppers, cover and cook for 15-20 minutes, depending on thickness.

Rice and Gandules

Yield: 6 Servings
Cooking Time: 30 minutes

1 onion, chopped

1 red pepper, deseeded, chopped

6 cloves garlic, minced

1 handful fresh cilantro, chopped

2 tablespoons extra virgin olive oil

1 packet Sazon

2 cups uncooked white rice

15 ounce can gandules peas, drained
   and juice reserved

3 cups chicken broth

¼ teaspoon Adobo seasoning

Salt to taste

Heat oil in a large saucepot over medium high heat. Add the onion, red pepper, garlic and cilantro and cook for about 8 minutes.

Add sazon and continue to cook for another 2 minutes. Add rice and cook stirring frequently for another 5 minutes. Add gandules and combine.

Put reserved juice from can of gandules peas in a measuring cup and add chicken broth and turn heat to high. Bring to a boil.

Add adobo and taste to make sure enough salt. If desired add salt a pinch at a time. Cover, reduce heat to medium low and cook for 20 minutes.

Shrimp Ceviche

Yield: 4-6 Servings
Cooking Time: 20 minutes

1.5 lbs. raw jumbo size shrimp	**1 tablespoon ketchup**
1 small onion, thinly sliced	**Garnishes:**
8 tablespoons lemon juice	**2 tomatoes, chopped**
3 tablespoons extra virgin olive oil	**1 avocado, chopped**
1 tablespoon salt	**1 bunch cilantro, chopped**

Cook shrimp in boiling water until it turns pink. Remove and rinse under cold water. Place in refrigerator for 15 minutes.

Meanwhile, rinse the onion slices with warm water. Combine the onions, lemon juice, oil and salt and let sit for approximately 10 minutes.

Combine cooked shrimp with the onion mixture and add ketchup. Add garnishes right before serving.

Note: You can add a dash of hot sauce for heat.

Simple Punch

Yield: 4 Servings
Cooking Time: 5 minutes

32 oz. cranberry juice
1 cup orange juice
1 cup pineapple juice

1 cup sprite or ginger ale
Optional: 3 oz. rum

Put all ingredients except the rum in a pitcher and stir to combine.

Add rum if desired and stir.

Sloppy Joes

Yield: 4-6 Servings
Cooking Time: 30 Minutes

2 tablespoons extra-virgin olive oil	**1 tablespoon sugar**
1 large onion, chopped	**3 tablespoons Worcestershire sauce**
1 small red pepper, seeded & chopped	**2 tablespoons red wine vinegar**
4 large cloves garlic	**1 ½ tablespoons Dijon mustard**
1 teaspoon dried marjoram	**1 tablespoon ketchup**
1 ½ lbs. ground turkey meat	**¼ teaspoon salt**
15 oz. can tomato sauce	**⅛ teaspoon pepper**

Heat the oil in a large skillet over medium high heat. Add the onions and red pepper and sauté for about 5 minutes, or until translucent.

Add the garlic and marjoram and continue to cook for another 2 minutes.

Add the ground turkey meat and cook until no longer pink, about 5 minutes, breaking up while it cooks.

Add the tomato sauce, sugar, Worcestershire, vinegar, mustard, ketchup, salt & pepper. Bring to a boil.

Simmer on medium high heat for about 15 minutes, or until most of the liquid is absorbed, stirring occasionally.

Serve on Sandwich Rolls.

Spaghetti and Shrimp

Yield: 4 Servings
Cooking Time: 15 minutes

½ box spaghetti

2 tablespoons extra virgin olive oil

1 onion, chopped

3 cloves garlic, chopped

¼ teaspoon crushed red pepper

14.5 ounce can diced tomatoes
  with juice

8 ounce can tomato sauce

½ teaspoon dried basil

12 ounces medium fresh shrimp,
  peeled and deveined

2 cups fresh spinach

½ cup shredded parmesan cheese

Cook spaghetti according to box directions.

Heat oil in a large skillet over medium high heat. Add onion and saute for about 5 minutes. Add garlic and crushed red pepper and saute for another minute.

Add the tomatoes, tomato sauce and basil and bring to a boil. Add shrimp, cover and simmer for 5 minutes until shrimp are cooked through.

Add the cooked pasta and spinach to the skillet and combine well.

Serve each portion with parmesan cheese sprinkled on top.

Spinach Fritters

Yield: 6 Servings
Cooking Time: 30 minutes

¼ cup extra virgin olive oil
15 oz. part skim Ricotta Cheese
½ cup shredded Mozzarella Cheese
½ cup Shredded Parmesan Cheese
1 pkg. frozen spinach, defrosted and
   squeezed of water

1 tsp. Garlic Salt
1 large Tomato, chopped
3 eggs, beaten
2 cups Italian breadcrumbs

Heat a medium skillet over medium high heat. Add oil to cover bottom of pan.

In a large bowl combine the ricotta, mozzarella, parmesan, spinach, garlic salt and tomato. Using a ¼ cup measure, scoop mixture and roll into balls. Roll in egg and then breadcrumbs to coat and pat down into patty shape. Fry in oil for 2-3 minutes per side and drain on paper towel.

Very Berry Pie

Yield: 10-12 Servings
Cooking Time: 1 Hour

1 Box refrigerated ready made pie crust, 2 come in a box
1 can cherry pie filling

12 ounces frozen mixed berries, defrosted and drained
½ cup brown sugar

Preheat oven to 350 degrees.

Spray an oven proof pie dish with no stick cooking spray. Roll out one of the pie crusts onto bottom of dish and prick all over with a fork. Bake in oven for 10 minutes.

In a medium bowl combine the canned cherries and the defrosted berries. Spread berry mixture evenly on top of pre-baked pie crust.

Top the pie with the other pie crust and again prick with fork all over. Sprinkle brown sugar over top and bake for 40 minutes.

Let cool for at least ½ hour before slicing.

White Chocolate Meringue Drops

Yield: 8-10 Servings
Cooking Time: 10 minutes...2 hours in oven

2 egg whites	**½ cup granulated sugar**
⅛ teaspoon salt	**6 ounce package white chocolate chips**
½ teaspoon cream of tartar	

Preheat oven to 375 degrees.

Beat egg whites until stiff with electric mixer (should take about 5 minutes). Gradually add salt, cream of tartar and sugar to egg whites. Add white chocolate chips and combine gently.

Drop by the teaspoon onto cookie sheet sprayed with nonstick cooking spray. Place in oven and turn oven off at once. Let stand in oven for at least 2 hours.

Acknowledgements

Jill K. Vallaro:

To my husband, Ron Vallaro, daughter, Carisa Lingenfelter, son-in-law, Bruce Lingenfelter, my grandson, Jake S. Lingenfelter, the Vallaro and Dease families, NY Presbyterian Hospital medical team, Dr. Joshua Sonett and staff, Dr. Mark Stoopler and staff, Columbia Doctors, my sister, Christine and brother-in-law, Rich F., my partners, Ilene V., and Yvette D., my great friends, Deborah P., Barbara M., Sandra H., Charlie R., Cindy D., Cheryl A., whom gave me overwhelming support, love and a vision to FADE THE COLORS OF CANCER.

Ilene Vazquez:

To my husband, David Vazquez, my two incredible sons Jacob and Nico, my family, my amazing friends, Northern Westchester Hospital and their staff, Dr. Rizzi and staff, Dr. Messina and staff, Dr. Close and staff, Dr. Gold and staff, my awesome chemo nurses Jess and Alaina, my partners Jill V. and Yvette D. I could have never made it without you!

Yvette Delgado:

To my husband Roland, my amazing kids Courtney, Kyle, Nicole. My family and friends. To my father, I couldn't have asked for a better dad. The team at Memorial Sloan Kettering, Dr. Peter Allen and staff, Dr. Nancy Sklarin and staff. My two girls, Ilene V, Jill V, thank you for holding my hand through this hard time and assuring me that it will be fine. It will never be forgotten.